Blairmore Municipal Library

D0566356

Where Animals Live

The World of Seals

Adapted from Doug Allan's *The Seal on the Rocks*

Words by
David Saintsing

Photographs by
Oxford Scientific Films

Gareth Stevens Publishing
Milwaukee

Contents

Note: The use of a capital letter for a seal's name means that is a specific *type* (or *species*) of seal (such as the Northern Elephant Seal). The use of a lower case, or small, letter for a seal's name means that it is a member of the larger *group* of seals.

Where Seals Live

Seals are *mammals* that spend much of their lives in water. Like people, seals are warm-blooded. Their bodies stay at the same temperature, even when they are in cold water.

The ancestors of seals lived completely on land, so they had legs and feet to walk on. The legs *evolved* into *flippers* over millions of years. Now seals are built for diving and swimming.

Seals can spend a long time in the water. Some *species* swim great distances to find food. Other kinds stay close to one stretch of land. All seals come ashore to have babies and to lie on the beach or on rocks. Thus seals live in two different types of *habitat*.

Seals Around the World

Seals live in many different places around the world. This Monk Seal lives on the warm beaches of Hawaii. One of the largest seals, the Elephant Seal, lives off the coasts of Mexico and California. Elephant Seals like to lie close together to help stay warm. They can be up to 14 ft (3.5 m) long.

Most seals live in the *temperate* and polar areas of the world. In these regions there is plenty of food.

Blairmore Municipal Library

Some seals, like these Harbor Seals, rest on rocks and beaches. Others prefer to rest in *estuaries* and bays.

Seals like to fish alone at sea. But on shore, they stay in large groups. These Southern Elephant Seals don't mind sharing their beach with penguins!

↑

The most common type of seal is the Crabeater. Scientists believe there are 30 million Crabeaters! They live on the ice *floes* of Antarctica and may never truly come ashore.

The Hooded Seal lives in the Arctic. It can inflate its nose when it is angry or scared.

↓

The Seal's Body

Seals spend some time on land, but they are better adapted for living in water. They have streamlined bodies which let them swim with little effort. They have a pair of flippers near the front and a pair right at the rear.

These flippers are arms and legs with skin growing between the fingers and toes as webbing.

Seals are warm-blooded. To help keep them warm they have a thick coat of fur and a layer of *blubber*. The blubber also helps seals float while they are in the water.

Seals come in a variety of colors. Most are gray or brown. Some are all one color. Others, like these Gray Seals, are spotted. Most seals are paler on their underside than on top. Their coloring is a form of *camouflage*.

The Seal's Head

This male Elephant Seal has a special use for his big nose! He can snort air into it and puff it out. This gives him a mating roar that is very loud. All seals have a good sense of smell. Their nostrils are at the tip of their nose. This is the best place for breathing in rough seas.

Seals also have good eyesight, and they are able to judge distances. This helps them chase fast-moving *prey*.

↑

A seal's face looks a lot like a dog's! Seals have long whiskers growing out of their cheeks. Their whiskers are very sensitive to touch and help seals find fish moving in the water.

Seals do not have outer ears. But they have good hearing. Without an outer ear, seals are more streamlined for swimming. All they have are small ear holes on each side of the head.

↓

How Seals Move in Water

↑

Seals are at home in the water. They float, dive, and swim in many directions. When swimming slowly, they use their front flippers to paddle along like the seal above.

Seals also use their front flippers to steer. You can see that the seal in the middle of the group (right) has its flippers stretched out to help it ➡ turn around.

When seals swim fast, their front flippers are held close to the body, and all of their power comes from the rear flippers. Seals are usually happy to cruise along slowly. But they can swim 15 mph (24 kph) if they have to.

Seals can hold their breath for a long time. Some, like this Elephant Seal (left), can stay underwater for an hour. Their bodies make changes to help use oxygen very slowly.

How Seals Move on Land

When seals are in the water, it takes little effort to move. But on land, seals have to work very hard to move. Flippers are not as useful as legs for walking.

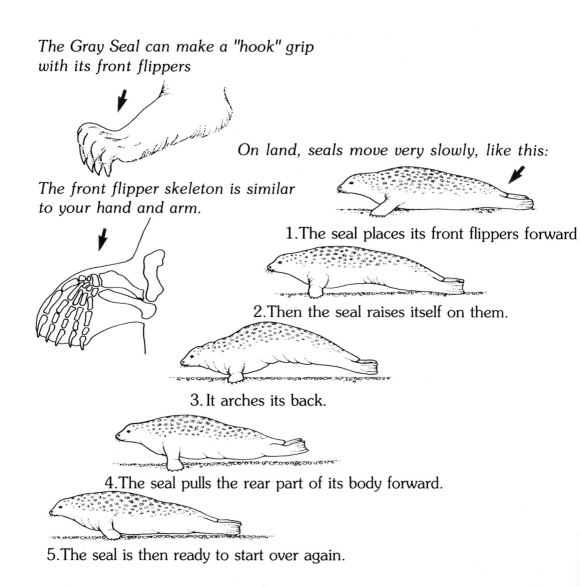

The Gray Seal can make a "hook" grip with its front flippers

The front flipper skeleton is similar to your hand and arm.

On land, seals move very slowly, like this:

1. The seal places its front flippers forward

2. Then the seal raises itself on them.

3. It arches its back.

4. The seal pulls the rear part of its body forward.

5. The seal is then ready to start over again.

↑

Some seals, like this young Gray Seal, can curl the tips of their flippers to help pull them along rocky shores.

Seals that live in the polar regions have it easier. They can slide across ice and snow. Crabeater Seals can move over ice at 15 mph (24 kph).

↓

Food and Feeding

All seals are *carnivorous*. Some eat many kinds
of food. Others have more limited diets.
Common and Gray Seals eat squid, octopus,
and many kinds of fish. Seals hunt by swimming
under schools of fish. They can look up and see
the fish against the light above.

Leopard Seals have extra large front flippers so
they can turn sharply as they chase penguins.

↓

Crabeater Seals that live around Antarctica eat
only *krill*. Krill are shrimp-like *crustaceans*.
Seals hunt krill just below the surface of the
water.

This Crabeater skull shows how the teeth strain
krill from the water. The seal pushes out the
water from inside its mouth. It then swallows
the krill that are left behind.

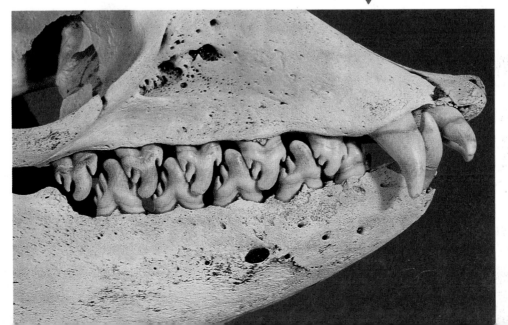

Coping with Heat and Cold

On warm days, seals sometimes stay cool by throwing wet gravel onto their backs. They also use their flippers like radiators to carry heat away from their bodies. Or they make many trips to the sea to keep their skin wet.

In cold weather, their layer of blubber helps keep seals warm.

Every year, seals lose their hair. This is called *molting.*

↑

Some seals, like these Elephant Seals, lose both their hair and their outer layer of skin. These seals like to lie in mud pools to soothe their itchy skin.

Seals in polar regions must get under the frozen winter seas to find food. Some go to places where the ice is broken up to get into the water. Others, like this Weddell Seal, bite holes through the ice with their teeth.

↓

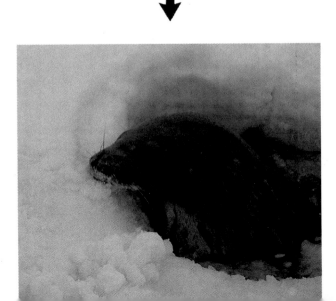

The Breeding Season

Young seals are called pups. They are usually born in the spring and summer, when the weather is good. To have their pups, seals come out of the water.

The birth of a pup takes only a minute or so. The three pictures above show the birth of a Weddell Seal pup. When it comes out of its mother (upper left), it may still be in the sac of fluid in which it has been developing (upper center). This sac breaks open after the seal is born (upper right).

After the mother breaks the *umbilical cord,* she smells her newborn pup. This smell will lead her to the pup when she returns from feeding trips.

With some kinds of seals, the males set up *territories* before the babies are born. These Elephant Seals are fighting for territory on the breeding beach. Because they have such thick skins, there are usually no serious injuries. ⬇

Rearing the Young

Seals protect their pups in different ways. This
Weddell Seal pup still has part of its umbilical
cord attached to it. Its mother stays with it all
the time for the first week or so. Then she
slowly gets it to go into the water and swim.
The mother Gray Seal leaves her pup while she
feeds at sea. She returns to feed the pup four
or five times the first day. After that, she may
return only twice a day. Each mother seal finds
her own pup by its cry and smell.

↑

Baby seals feed on their mothers' milk. The milk is very rich, and the pups grow fast. It takes from three weeks to two months after birth for pups to be *weaned* from their mothers' milk.

This Gray Seal pup is weaned and is molting its baby coat of hair. It now feeds itself, and it will wander far in its early years of life. In time, it will settle down along one stretch of coastline.

↓

Enemies and Defense

In the frozen Arctic, adult seals are hunted on the ice floes by Polar Bears. The bears sometimes creep up on sleeping seals and grab them before the seals can escape into the water. Or they may crouch by the seals' breathing holes and lift the seals onto the ice when they come up for air.

Adult seals that live in warmer regions are safe from natural *predators* on land.

In the water, seals use their speed to escape predators. In the Arctic, they can easily outswim Polar Bears. Some, however, fall prey to Killer Whales. In warmer waters, seals may be eaten by sharks.

Down in the Antarctic, Leopard Seals like the one below hunt young Crabeater Seals. After the Crabeater pups have been weaned, they leave their mothers. That is when Leopard Seals become a danger to them.

Seals and People

↑

These Crabeaters seem eager to meet a scientific diver underwater! The scientist below is putting a numbered tag on a pup's flipper. This is one way of learning if the seal returns to its birthplace when it breeds as an adult.

Not all contact with people has been so friendly, however. People have hunted seals for food throughout history, and Harp Seal pups have been hunted for their white *pelts.* ➡

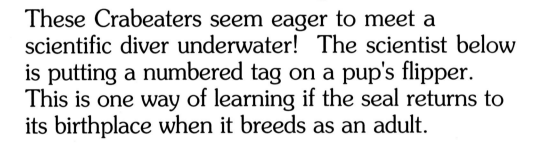

Some people feel there are so many seals that hunting them won't harm their numbers. But many feel that seals should not be killed so rich people can have fancy coats. Laws have been passed protecting seals from hunters during the breeding season. But laws have also been passed letting fishermen kill seals that get into fishing nets. Today, seal pelts cannot be sold in Europe or the US. Also, the Canadian government is thinking of banning all killing of seals.

Friends, Neighbors, and Two Close Relatives

Many animals live with seals. Penguins share the ice floes in Antarctica. In both polar areas, seals and whales feed together on shrimp.

Two animals, the Sea-lion and the Walrus, are very close relatives of the seal. Walruses live in the Arctic. Sea-lions live in parts of Antarctica and the Pacific Ocean. Sea-lions in cold parts of the world have thick, coarse hair. These Sea-lions are called Fur Seals. ⬇

This Hooker's Sea-lion lives south of New Zealand. Sea-lions look a lot like seals, but their hind flippers bend beneath their bodies. This makes them quicker than seals on land. Unlike seals, Sea-lions do not use their rear flippers for swimming. Also, Sea-lions have ear flaps.

Walruses are very big relatives of the seal! They weigh over one ton. They have long *tusks* with which they dig up clams for food. Walruses like to live in large herds.

Life on the Rocks

3 1817 00954 6755

The drawing below shows that seals get their energy from certain sea animals. And in turn, other animals eat seals, either as predators or as *scavengers* that feed on the bodies of dead seals. These animals are part of a food chain, and they depend on one another for their survival.

Food Chain

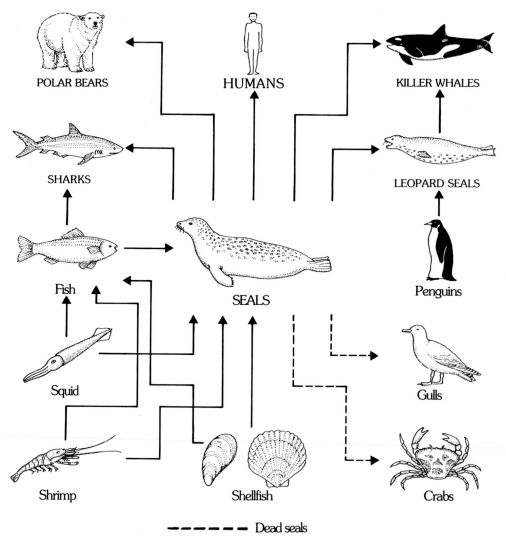

POLAR BEARS   HUMANS   KILLER WHALES

SHARKS   LEOPARD SEALS

Fish   SEALS   Penguins

Squid   Gulls

Shrimp   Shellfish   Crabs

– – – – – – Dead seals

Like this Gray Seal, seals are nicely adapted for their life in the water. But they are also tied to the land for their breeding and molting. Most seals live safe lives. But it is here, on land, that they are most in danger from humans.

In some parts of the world, we threaten seals by hunting them and spoiling their habitats. We can protect these fascinating animals by passing laws that save them and by protecting their habitats from *pollution.*

Index and New Words About Seals

These new words about seals appear in the text on the pages shown after each definition. Each new word first appears in the text in *italics*, just as it appears here.

Reading level analysis: SPACHE 2.5, FRY 2, FLESCH 98 (very easy), RAYGOR 4, FOG 4, SMOG 3

Library of Congress Cataloging-in-Publication Data
Saintsing, David.
  The world of seals.
  (Where animals live)
  "Adapted from Doug Allan's The seal on the rocks."
  Includes index.
  Summary: Simple text and photographs depict seals feeding, breeding, and defending themselves in their natural habitats.
  1. Seals (Animals)--Juvenile literature. [1. Seals (Animals)] I. Allan, Douglas. The seal on the rocks. II. Oxford Scientific Films. III. Title. IV. Series.
QL737.P6S25 1988   599.74'8   87-6524
ISBN 1-55532-325-1   ISBN 1-55532-300-6 (lib. bdg.)

North American edition first published in 1988 by
Gareth Stevens, Inc.
7221 West Green Tree Road Milwaukee, WI 53223, USA
US edition, this format, copyright ©1988 by Belitha Press Ltd.
Text copyright © 1988 by Gareth Stevens, Inc.

All rights reserved. No part of this book may be reproduced in any form or by any means without permission in writing from Gareth Stevens, Inc. First conceived, designed, and produced by Belitha Press Ltd., London, as **The Seal on the Rocks**, with an original text copyright by Oxford Scientific Films. Format copyright by Belitha Press Ltd.

Typeset in Milwaukee by Web Tech, Inc. Printed in Hong Kong by South China Printing Co.
Series Editor: Mark J. Sachner. Art Director: Treld Bicknell.
Design: Naomi Games. Cover Design: Gary Moseley. Line Drawings: Lorna Turpin.
Scientific Consultants: Gwynne Vevers and David Saintsing.

The publishers wish to thank the following for permission to reproduce copyright photographs: **Doug Allan** for pp. 6 below, 7 above, 8 below, 10, 12 below, 13, 17 above, 18, 19 both, 22, 23 above, 24 below, 25, 26 above, and front cover; pp. 20 below and 21 above (photographer Ken Richard). **Oxford Scientific Films Ltd.** for pp. 8 above, 12, and title page (photographer Martyn Chillmaid); pp. 2 and back cover (photographer Robin Redfern); pp. 3 and 23 below (photographer Tony Martin); p. 4 (photographer Maurice Tibbles); p. 5 (photographer E.R. Degginger); pp. 6 above and 29 (photographer Leonard Lee Rue III); pp. 7 below, 15 below, 21 below, 27, and 28 below (photographer T.S. McCann); p. 9 (photographer Jacki Sime); p. 11 above (photographer Micheal Brooke); p. 11 below (photographer Tony Tilford); p. 15 above (photographer Peter O'Toole); p. 17 below (photographer C.J. Gilbert); p. 24 (photographer Hugh Miles); p. 31 (photographers David and Sue Cayless).

1 2 3 4 5 6 7 8 9 93 92 91 90 89 88

J599.74
SAI

026359

Blairmore Municipal Library

Blairmore Municipal Library

This book may be kept until last date
stamped below.

~~A fine of 15 cents per week will be
imposed for each week the book is~~
overdue

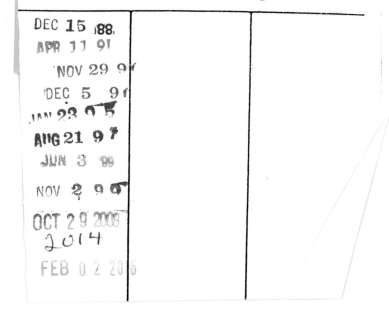

DEC 15 88		
APR 11 91		
NOV 29 91		
DEC 5 91		
JAN 23 95		
AUG 21 97		
JUN 3 99		
NOV 2 95		
OCT 29 2008		
2014		
FEB 0 2 2016		